A CENTURY *of*
STOCKTON-ON-TEES

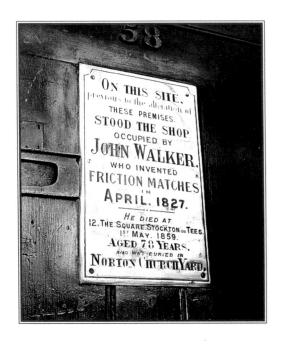

Will Hay was one of Stockton's favourite sons. He was born in a terraced house, 23 Durham Street, off Bishopton Lane, on 6 December 1888. His birth was registered at Stockton registry office on 18 January 1889.

> Every night when the moon shines bright, The miller's ghost is seen.
> He walks the track with a sack on his back, And his earhole painted green.

With this snatch of verse Will Hay's sceptical stationmaster, Mr Porter, deflates Moore Marriott's morbid retelling of the ghostly couplet about One-Eyed Joe, the miller, in the famous Gaumont British comedy *Oh, Mr Porter* made in 1938. This was his most acclaimed film; but he best loved playing variations of an incompetent, seedy schoolmaster.

A CENTURY *of*
STOCKTON-ON-TEES

CHARLIE EMETT

The
History
Press

First published in 1999 by Sutton Publishing Limited

This new paperback edition first published in 2007 by Sutton Publishing

Reprinted in 2009 by
The History Press
The Mill, Brimscombe Port,
Stroud, Gloucestershire, GL5 2QG
www.thehistorypress.co.uk

British Library Cataloguing in Publication Data
A catalogue record for this book is available from the British Library.

ISBN 978-0-7509-4910-1

Front endpaper: This aerial view of Stockton-on-Tees highlights the width of its High Street.
Back endpaper: Dunedin House, 28 October 1994. This is a prestige Stockton office development, built for the future for people like these two Stockton boys who are the future. Between them the Tees; before them the millennium.
Half title page: John Walker was born at 104 High Street, Stockton, on 29 May 1781. He was the inventor of the friction match. This plaque is on the doorway of the premises in Stockton High Street where he worked. A favourite son of Stockton, he died in 1859.
Title page: Ivy Close was the daughter of the manager of Samuel's Jewellery in Stockton and had two brothers and a sister. In 1908, when the *Daily Mirror* organised the first-ever national beauty contest to counter American claims that the best-looking women lived on their side of the Atlantic, Ivy was one of 15,000 hopefuls to enter, despite opposition from her father, who changed his mind when she won. She was dubbed 'the most beautiful woman in Britain'.

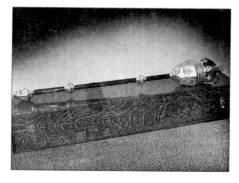

Typeset in Photina.
Typesetting and origination by
Sutton Publishing.
Printed and bound in England by
Athenaeum Press Ltd.

The mace, ceremonial staff of office of Stockton-on-Tees, carried by the mace-bearer in processions or ceremonies.

Contents

The Stockton and Darlington Railway was officially opened on 27 September 1825, when Locomotive No. 1 hauled twenty-six wagons and a coach the 21 miles from near West Auckland to Stockton, the remaining six wagons leaving the procession at Darlington. The opening set the pattern for the development of a railway system that would spread worldwide. At the beginning of the twentieth century, and with the age of steam at its height, Stockton's railway station, shown here, is indeed a very busy place.

Ropner Park was built on land donated by the Ropner family and opened to the public on 4 October 1883, by the Duke and Duchess of York who later became King George V and Queen Mary. The park's lake is pictured here at the beginning of the twentieth century.

Foreword

As the millennium approaches I would like to thank Mr Emett for taking the time to write an account of how the Borough of Stockton-on-Tees has changed for the better throughout the twentieth century. Let us hope that the next millennium sees even greater advances.

Councillor Mrs Jean Kitchen
The Worshipful the Mayor of the
Borough of Stockton-on-Tees (1999–2000)

The worshipful the Mayor of Stockton-on-Tees, Cllr Mrs Jean Kitchen.

Stockton High Street in the early 1900s.

Britain: A Century
of Change

Children gathered around an early wireless set in the 1920s. The speed
and forms of communication were to change dramatically as the century
advanced. (*Barnaby's Picture Library*)

The delirious rejoicing at the news of the Relief of Mafeking, during the Boer War in May 1900, is a colourful historical moment. But, in retrospect, the introduction that year of the first motor bus was rather more important, signalling another major adjustment to town life. In the previous 60 years railway stations, post-and-telegraph offices, police and fire stations, gas works and gasometers, new livestock markets and covered markets, schools, churches, football grounds, hospitals and asylums, water pumping stations and sewerage plants had totally altered the urban scene, as the country's population tripled and over 70 per cent were born in or moved to the towns.

When Queen Victoria died in 1901, she was measured for her coffin by her grandson Kaiser Wilhelm, the London prostitutes put on black mourning and the blinds came down in the villas and terraces spreading out from the old town centres. These centres were reachable by train and tram, by the new bicycles and still newer motor cars, con-nected by the new telephone, and lit by gas or even electricity. The shops may have been full of British-made cotton and woollen clothing but the grocers and butchers were selling cheap Danish bacon, Argentinian beef, Australasian mutton, tinned or dried fish and fruit from Canada, California and South Africa. Most of these goods were carried in British-built-and-crewed ships, burning Welsh steam coal.

As the first decade moved on, the Open Spaces Act meant more parks, bowling greens and cricket pitches. The first state pensions came in, together with higher taxation and death duties. These were raised mostly to pay for the new Dreadnought battleships needed to maintain naval superiority over Germany, and deter them from war. But the deterrent did not work. The First World War transformed the place of women, as they took over many men's jobs. Its other legacies were the war memorials which joined the statues of Victorian worthies in main squares round the land. After 1918 death duties bit even harder and a quarter of England changed hands in a few years.

Women working as porters on the Great Western Railway, Paddington, *c.* 1917. (*W.L. Kenning/ Adrian Vaughan Collection*)

The multiple shop – the chain store – appeared in the high street: Sainsburys, Maypole, Lipton's, Home & Colonial, the Fifty Shilling Tailor, Burton, Boots, W.H. Smith. The shopper was spoilt for choice, attracted by the brash fascias and advertising hoardings for national brands like

Bovril, Pears Soap, and Ovaltine. Many new buildings began to be seen, such as garages, motor showrooms, picture palaces (cinemas), 'palais de dance', and the bow-windowed, pebble-dashed, tile-hung, half-timbered houses that were built as ribbon-development along the roads and new bypasses or on the new estates nudging the green belts.

During the 1920s cars became more reliable and sophisticated as well as commonplace, with developments like the electric self-starter making them easier for women to drive. Who wanted to turn a crank handle in the new short skirt? This was, indeed, the electric age as much as the motor era. Trolley buses, electric trams and trains extended mass transport and electric light replaced gas in the street and the home, which itself was groomed by the vacuum cleaner.

A major jolt to the march onward and upward was administered by the Great Depression of the early 1930s. The older British industries – textiles, shipbuilding, iron, steel, coal – were already under pressure from foreign competition when this worldwide slump arrived, cutting exports by half in two years and producing 3 million unemployed (and still rising) by 1932. Luckily there were new diversions to alleviate the misery. The 'talkies' arrived in the cinemas; more and more radios and gramophones were to be found in people's homes; there were new women's magazines, with fashion, cookery tips and problem pages; football pools; the flying feats of women pilots like Amy Johnson; the Loch Ness Monster; cheap chocolate and the drama of Edward VIII's abdication.

Father and child cycling past Buckingham Palace on VE Day, 8 May 1945. (*Hulton Getty Picture Collection*)

Things were looking up again by 1936 and unemployment was down to 2 million. New light industry was booming in the Home Counties as factories struggled to keep up with the demand for radios, radiograms, cars and electronic goods including the first television sets. The threat from Hitler's Germany meant rearmament, particularly of the airforce, which stimulated aircraft and aero engine firms. If you were lucky and lived in the south, there was good money to be earned. A semi-detached house cost £450, a Morris Cowley £150. People may have smoked like chimneys but life expectancy, since 1918, was up by 15 years while the birth rate had almost halved. The fifty-four hour week was down to forty-eight hours and there were 9 million radio licences by 1939.

In some ways it is the little memories that seem to linger longest from the Second World War: the kerbs painted white to show up in the

A family gathered around their television set in the 1950s. (*Hulton Getty Picture Collection*)

blackout, the rattle of ack-ack shrapnel on roof tiles, sparrows killed by bomb blast, painting your legs brown and then adding a black seam down the back to simulate stockings. The biggest damage, apart from London, was in the south-west (Plymouth, Bristol) and the Midlands (Coventry, Birmingham). Postwar reconstruction was rooted in the Beveridge Report which set out the expectations for the Welfare State. This, together with the nationalisation of the Bank of England, coal, gas, electricity and the railways, formed the programme of the Labour government in 1945. At this time the USA was calling in its debts and Britain was beggared by the war, yet still administering its Empire.

Times were hard in the late 1940s, with rationing even more stringent than during the war. Yet this was, as has been said, 'an innocent and well-behaved era'. The first let-up came in 1951 with the Festival of Britain and then there was another fillip in 1953 from the Coronation.

which incidentally gave a huge boost to the spread of TV. By 1954 leisure motoring had been resumed but the Comet – Britain's best hope for taking on the American aviation industry – suffered a series of mysterious crashes. The Suez debacle of 1956 was followed by an acceleration in the withdrawal from Empire, which had begun in 1947 with the Independence of India. Consumerism was truly born with the advent of commercial TV and most homes soon boasted washing machines, fridges, electric irons and fires.

The *Lady Chatterley* obscenity trial in 1960 was something of a straw in the wind for what was to follow in that decade. A collective loss of inhibition seemed to sweep the land, as stately home owners opened up, the Beatles and the Rolling Stones transformed popular music, and retailing, cinema and the theatre were revolutionised. Designers, hairdressers, photographers and models moved into places vacated by an Establishment put to flight by the new breed of satirists spawned by *Beyond the Fringe* and *Private Eye*.

In the 1970s Britain seems to have suffered a prolonged hangover after the excesses of the previous decade. Ulster, inflation and union troubles were not made up for by entry into the EEC, North Sea Oil, Women's Lib or, indeed, Punk Rock. Mrs Thatcher applied the corrective in the 1980s, as the country moved more and more from its old manufacturing base over to providing services, consulting, advertising, and expertise in the 'invisible' market of high finance or in IT. Britain entertained the world with *Cats*, *Phantom of the Opera*, *Four Weddings and a Funeral*, *The Full Monty*, *Mr Bean* and the *Teletubbies*.

The post-1945 townscape has seen changes to match those in the worlds of work, entertainment and politics. In 1956 the Clean Air Act served notice on smogs and pea-souper fogs, smuts and blackened buildings, forcing people to stop burning coal and go over to smokeless sources of heat and energy. In the same decade some of the best urban building took place in the 'new towns' like Basildon, Crawley, Stevenage and Harlow. Elsewhere open warfare was declared on slums and what was labelled inadequate, cramped, back-to-back, two-up, two-down, housing. The new 'machine for living in' was a flat in a high-rise block. The architects and planners who promoted these were in league with the traffic engineers,

Carnaby Street in the 1960s. (*Barnaby's Picture Library*)

13

The Millennium Dome at Greenwich, 1999. (*Michael Durnan/Barnaby's Picture Library*)

determined to keep the motor car moving whatever the price in multi-storey car parks, meters, traffic wardens and ring roads.

The old pollutant, coal smoke, was replaced by petrol and diesel exhaust, and traffic noise. Even in the back garden it was hard to find peace as motor mowers, then leaf blowers and strimmers made themselves heard, and the neighbours let you share their choice of music from their powerful new amplifiers, whether you wanted to or not. Fast food was no longer only a pork pie in a pub or fish-and-chips. There were Indian curry houses, Chinese take-aways and American-style hamburgers, while the drinker could get away from beer in a wine bar. Under the impact of television the big Gaumonts and Odeons closed or were rebuilt as multi-screen cinemas, while the palais de dance gave way to discos and clubs.

From the late 1960s the introduction of listed buildings and conservation areas, together with the growth of preservation societies, put a brake on 'comprehensive redevelopment'. Now the new risk at the end of the 1990s is that town centres may die, as shoppers are attracted to the edge-of-town supermarkets surrounded by parking space, where much more than food and groceries can be bought. The ease of the one-stop shop represents the latest challenge to the good health of our towns. But with care, ingenuity and a determination to keep control of our environment, this challenge can be met.

Stockton-on-Tees: An Introduction

The dawn of a new century, 1 January 1900, and Victoria was still on the throne. Great Britain's imperial powers had never been greater and its Empire, on which the sun never set, had, as the *Northern Echo* reported, 'one heart, one head, one language and one policy'.

Some of the people of Stockton-on-Tees viewed the turn of the century differently. Most of them were proud of Great Britain's dominion over lands which stretched around the globe but they wondered why none of the benefits accrued from the overseas dependencies reached them. Actually they did, obliquely, through commerce and trade, but this meant little to people living in squalor.

By the early nineteenth century, Stockton's future lay in the hands of its merchants and craftsmen, enterprising people who promoted and financed many innovative schemes. As the Industrial Revolution developed, some ironworks were established in Stockton, but Middlesbrough, across the River Tees, was *the* iron town. Stockton was more diversified: foundry work, marine and locomotive engineering and shipbuilding. Stockton remained a regional market town with a large professional and commercial middle-class population.

Stockton slid into the new century to the tune of Elgar's *Gerontius*, written in 1900. The following year Victoria died and Edward VII reigned for the rest of the decade.

Edwardian Stockton was a town of great contrasts. The leading citizens, usually well-heeled members of local society, relaxed with proper propriety and indulged in genteel pursuits. To be seen regularly at worship was important both for the good of the soul and as an example to the lower orders, many of whom lived in slums on either side of the High Street, the widest in the land.

Many Stockton workmen were employed in foundries or shipyards on the south bank of the Tees. They crossed the river on Kelley's Ferry and the fare was never increased more than ½d per passenger. For many years Stockton remained the lowest bridging point on the Tees; and for decades steamers travelled between Stockton and Middlesbrough until the arrival of trams.

In 1900 Stockton was well endowed with churches, chapels and schools. It had a public library, opened in 1877, a fire station built in 1883 to replace horse-drawn equipment and a new hospital, built in the late 1870s at Bowesfield Lane to supplement the smaller one already there.

Two events took place in 1912, both of which affected Stockton. On her maiden voyage, SS *Titanic* struck an iceberg on 14 April and sank. One of the passengers was W.T. Stead, the first editor of the *Northern Echo*. He was an outstanding newspaperman and his death was a great loss to *Northern Echo* readers, many of whom lived in Stockton. That same year F.W. Woolworth and Co. was founded: later a branch was opened in Stockton.

Stockton and Thornaby Hospital, built at a cost of just over £9,000, was adjacent to Bowesfield Lane and replaced Stockton Surgical Hospital. It originally accommodated 35 patients, the first of whom were admitted in 1877. A wing was added in 1890 and in 1926 Princess Mary opened a further extension, increasing the accommodation to 130 beds. The hospital was demolished in 1977.

In 1913 songwriter Jack Judge wrote 'Tipperary' and for the next four years Stockton men, fired with patriotism, went to war singing it. Many never returned from this war to end wars that experts predicted 'would be over by Christmas'. They were slaughtered in the mud of Mons and Ypres. During the conflict regular recruiting drives for the armed forces were held in Stockton, industrial output was increased and women moved into previously male-dominated jobs.

The war ended with food shortages which led to the establishment of food kitchens and rationing in Stockton as elsewhere. Following the Armistice the populace embarked on a decade of fun. The 1920s became known as a flighty decade. A new dance, the tango, came to Stockton, hemlines rose and the latest vogues favoured a lighter look. In 1921 short frocks came into fashion and patrons watching Charlie Chaplin's first full-length film *The Kid* sucked Fox's new glacier mints.

But living conditions in certain parts of Stockton deteriorated to such an extent by the early 1920s that a slum clearance programme was initiated. At long last the town's poorest inhabitants could see light at the end of the tunnel; the Englishman's dream fulfilled, a decent place of their own in which to live. For many it remained a dream: two unrelated events saw to that.

The first occurred on 12 November 1923 in Munich, when Adolf Hitler jumped on to a chair, fired a shot at the ceiling and shouted 'The National Revolution has begun'. The second happened in 1926. The miners went on strike and the TUC called a General Strike of essential services in sympathy. The strike lasted for nine days but coal shortages continued into the following year.

Between the two, in 1924, Stockton got a new medical officer, Dr G.C.M. M'Gonigle, who reduced both the infant mortality rate and the number of crippled children in the town through his orthopaedic work. In the local schools a third of a pint of milk was available at 1d per bottle, complete with a hygienic straw for making slurping noises.

Now straight dresses without waistlines were in, skirts were back above the knee and cloche hats were requisite. 'Yes, We Have No Bananas' was the latest song and it caught the flavour of the early 1920s. In Stockton there was a boom in hairdressing as women rushed to shingle their hair.

On 24 October 1929, Black Thursday, the Wall Street Crash in New York had worldwide repercussions. Its effect on Stockton was devastating. Shipyards closed and many jobs were lost. Escapism hit new heights both at Stockton's cinemas where Laurel and Hardy comedies played to full houses, and in fashion, where skirts were back below the knee and dresses were showing a softer, more feminine line. A popular song of 1932, 'Let's Have Another Cup of Coffee', expressed the philosophical outlook of many people at this depressive time.

During the 1930s ICI Ltd became established at nearby Billingham bringing much-needed employment to Teesside. Several road reconstructions were embarked upon to improve communications in and around Stockton.

By 1938, however, war clouds were gathering. Mr Chamberlain, having signed a non-aggression pact with Hitler, proclaimed 'peace in our time'; but he knew that time was running out. The following year, newspaper boys in Stockton and elsewhere whistled a new, escapist song, 'South of the Border'. On 3 September 1939, Britain declared war on Germany, and Stockton had its corporate hands full.

War changes everything. Conscription included both sexes and the whole population was involved one way or another. Railings were removed for conversion into shells, people dug for victory, the blackout was strictly observed, rationing was introduced and anti-gossip posters appeared: 'Careless Talk Costs Lives'; 'Be Like Dad – Keep Mum'.

Germany capitulated on 7 May and Japan surrendered on 14 August 1945. Stockton got lit up actually and metaphorically and Stocktonians began getting used to there being 'a peace on'.

On 12 February 1947, Britain suffered heavy snowstorms with sub-zero temperatures, its worst winter since 1894.

By the early 1950s four out of five Stockton people were within reach of a television set, the box in the corner. With the advent of TV, cinema receipts plummeted; but the big screen moguls retaliated with musicals like *Singin' in the Rain*, a classic example of Hollywood production at its best. The film was shown in Stockton in 1952 when

Gene Kelly thrilled cinema-goers by dancing through a downpour on electrifying feet. It was a classic performance.

Ladies' footwear fashion hit a dangerous ultra-high in 1953 with the introduction of stiletto heels. Many a Stockton lass sprained her ankle on stilettos and countless floors were damaged.

For many years English home interiors were of the traditional chintzy 'lived in' look. In 1958, designers were advocating clean-cut, angular lines and contemporary furniture became popular. Even more popular were family holidays at Butlins 'where you can make new friends'. A great many Stockton people did just that.

During the 1960s Stockton's boundaries continued to spread north and west towards Norton and Egglescliffe. New housing and shopping area developments changed the town centre, but some distinctive and important buildings remained to preserve Stockton's appearance as a market and business centre.

In 1963 the Beatles recorded their first LP, *Please Please Me*, and it sold well in Stockton. Alfred Hitchcock's *The Birds* and the first James Bond film, *Dr No*, thrilled Stockton picture-goers, flower power arrived and the town's many pubs did good business. In 1968 the mini-skirt reached such heights that cleaners charged by the inch!

In 1970, Oxford and Cambridge University Press published one million copies of the New English Bible and the entire output was sold out almost at once. Two well-beloved Stockton bookshops, W.H. Smith and Dressers, had excellent sales.

Mrs Thatcher visited Teesside in 1987 with a mission to spread a little southern affluence to areas like Teesside where the need was greatest. Critics questioned whether lost jobs would ever be replaced because the traditional heavy industries were dying on their feet. She launched the Teesside Development Corporation, a body charged with reinvigorating the area. It was a formidable task but the will to make a success of it was there. TDC Chairman, Ron Norman, summed it up: 'People from Leeds, Newcastle and even London will be coming to Teesside because of the facilities which will be there.'

Today a revitalised Stockton, which once backed on to the Tees, now turns its front to it. On the eve of the millennium Stocktonians enthuse about Stockton's 'miracle': the £50 million Tees barrage, which is making the town attractive to industrialists, businesspeople and sportsmen and women alike. With it, TDC has produced a model others are eager to follow, and given Stockton the means to stride confidently into the twenty-first century.

The First Decade

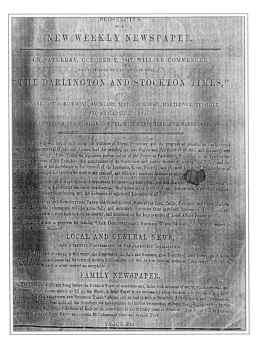

Famed as a market town serving a large, multiform population, part urban but mainly rural, Stockton needed a newspaper that would be readily acceptable to such a diverse readership. On Saturday 2 October 1847, that need was fulfilled; and more than 150 years later, this splendid weekly newspaper sells 32,000 copies a week over a wide area including the Yorkshire Dales, the North York Moors, the Vale of York, rural Durham, Cleveland and Stockton itself. The *D & S*, as it is popularly known in its North Yorkshire heartland, is one of the last newspapers in the country to have retained the ultra-traditional format. Today it has news on the front page, but until 3 October 1997, when it celebrated its 150th anniversary, it carried only advertisements on page 1. The only time this tradition was broken was to carry the result of the Richmond by-election, won by William Hague.

The changing face of the *Darlington & Stockton Times* over more than 150 years. The fourth version from the top is the one that was in use in 1909. The paper has always sought to provide a thorough and concise digest of the week's news. The paper is especially proud of its local government reports but its speciality has always been its agricultural content.

Stockton's Literary and Philosophical Institute was built in the 1860s and would have been a familiar sight to townspeople at the beginning of the century. It became the premises of the *Northern Echo* until it was purchased in 1964 by an unidentified developer. The *Northern Echo* offices then moved to nearby Nelson Terrace.

Stockton High Street at the turn of the century with the electric tramlines and a market for farm implements.

Electric tram drivers, Stockton, c. 1900. The tramway, or street railway, was a track of grooved rails laid flush with the road surface on which passenger tramcars were run. It was developed in the USA in the 1830s and imported to England in 1860. The early tramcars were horsedrawn. Stockton's first trams were steam driven but these were replaced by electric trams in 1898. Working a frequent service, with low fares, the electric tram was very popular during the early years of the twentieth century before coming into competition with the motor bus.

At the end of a day's toil in the harsh and less than salubrious conditions of Stockton's Quayside in about 1900 many workers found solace, and sometimes oblivion, in nearby taverns.

One such tavern stood proud of dismal Cleveland Row terrace at 17 Quayside. It was the Ship Launch Inn, pictured here in 1928, a year before it was demolished.

Many seeking refuge through alcohol became trapped in the desperate world of dipsomania from where, to their befuddled minds, oblivion was the only escape. To many, they were the dregs of society and beyond help: yet some saw them as unfortunates who needed help. These benefactors belonged to a movement of total abstainers, the Rechabites, dedicated people who held annual Band of Hope demonstrations and worked selflessly rehabilitating drunks and warning about the 'demon drink'. Here, in about 1900, members of the Stockton branch of the Rechabites are at a local Band of Hope gathering.

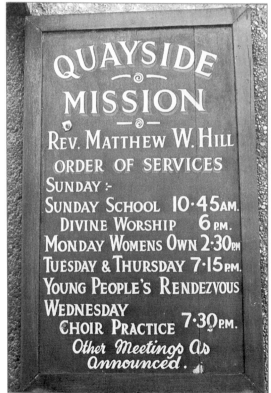

Where the Rechabites concentrated on the evils of drink, the Quayside Mission embraced all who wished to worship there. The notice-board, shown here in 1906, details its sacred and secular activities.

Bringing the geese to Stockton Market, 1902. At the turn of the century, this was a much more involved business than it is today. The geese had to be walked from the farms where they were bred and, since this was hard on their webbed feet, their owners provided them with 'shoes', a covering of tar that helped prevent the feet from wear and tear en route. Sheepdogs were used during the drive, working them as with sheep, and it was important not to 'clash' the geese as this would cause weight loss and affect the sale price.

Selling salmon in Stockton Market, 1902. At this time the Tees was a good salmon river and most, if not all, of the salmon shown in this picture would have been caught locally. This happy situation remained until around 1920 when the Tees became seriously affected by industrial pollution. Today salmon has returned to Stockton – I bought some at a local stall and it said so on the tin!

The Stockton Cherry Fair had very ancient origins going well back into the eighteenth century and earlier. The races were held on 18 July every year, about the time the cherries ripened, and a clerk of the sports was appointed to manage the various events. This picture was taken at the old Victoria Football Ground in 1904; the donkey races are about to start.

In 1908 the hugely popular operetta, *The Merry Widow*, with music by Franz Lehar and words by Adrian Ross, was presented at Stockton's Castle Theatre, direct from Daly's Theatre, London.

Also in 1908 Ivy Close, having won the first national beauty contest, fell in love with one of the *Daily Mirror*'s photographers, Elwin Neame, who had been sent by the paper to take her picture. Ivy was a typical English beauty, 5 ft 4 in tall with fair hair and blue eyes. She captivated Elwin and in 1912 they married. Elwin, engrossed with the silver screen, made a silent movie of her which so impressed British producer Cecil Hepworth that he set up Close Productions. In 1914 Ivy made her first feature film, *The Lure of London* and in 1916 signed a deal with the famous Kalem Comedy Co. in Florida, then America's movie capital. On Saturday 13 May of that year she sailed for New York. Ivy appeared in about 45 films but gave up in 1922, at Elwin's request, to look after their sons. In 1923 Elwin was killed in a motorcycle accident, leaving her almost destitute. She tried to revive her career, but by 1930 was reduced to playing bit parts. She returned to England and lived 'in the depths of poverty in a Bayswater flat'. Under the headline, 'Stockton Girl Cursed By Beauty', the *Gazette* commented that beauty 'had once again proved itself a curse rather than a blessing'. Ivy Neame died on 4 December 1968 at Goring-on-Thames.

Her son, Ronald Neame, became a leading director and producer whose classic films include *In Which We Serve*, *Brief Encounter* and *The Prime of Miss Jean Brodie*.

The southern end of Stockton High Street, *c.* 1909, with the Town Hall holding centre stage. The mile-long High Street is the widest in England and Stockton Castle once stood at its southern end. The Town Hall, constructed in 1735, was probably built with stone from the demolished castle. Note the horse drawn carriages on the right where some idea of the original shops' façades on the east side of the High Street can also be seen.

This close-up of the Victorian building glimpsed to the right of the above picture was taken in 1963. The ground floor façades have changed with the times but the remainder of the building illustrates the very high architectural standards achieved when it was built.

Two Stockton churches which look, today, much as they would have done in the first decade of the century. The impressive style of Holy Trinity Church (above) is highlighted in this view of its southern side. Photographed in 1993, the church was built on land granted by the Bishop of Durham in 1832. Holy Trinity was opened in 1838. Stockton parish church (below), in the High Street, was one of three Anglican churches in the centre of the town at the turn of the century. The other two were Holy Trinity in Yarm Lane and St John's in Alma Street, near the gasworks. Sited at the northern end of the High Street, Stockton parish church, a replacement for a chapel of ease, took two years to build. Work began in 1710 and the church was consecrated on 21 August 1712. The chancel was rebuilt in 1906 and a side chapel was added in 1925. The war memorial was built in 1923.

The First World War

Stockton Market in the High Street, with pedestrians perambulating
peacefully. 1912. The calm before the storm.

The First World War was very intense and differed from previous conflicts in that its progress was not dictated by either the seasons or the weather. It was the first time the major killer was war wounds, not disease. Many soldiers spent only short periods on the Western Front, usually because of wounds, and individuals often served in several theatres of war. Yet, despite these varying experiences, it was the trenches that became the unifying element of the war, which in reality was a diverse and multifaceted conflict. The trenches shown here have been preserved for posterity at the Hill 62 Museum in France. Many Stockton men ended their lives in trenches like this one.

The trench system in the Ypres sector was almost on top of the forward German positions. Here infantrymen have left the trenches and are advancing across no-man's-land towards enemy lines.

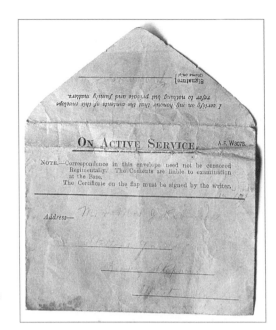

The last letter of private George Robinson of Kirkby Stephen, the author's home town, who was eighteen years old when he was killed as his company charged the Turkish positions on 21 August 1915.

Other Stockton men joined the Royal Navy and many served on ships of the Home Fleet. This scene shows ships of the Home Fleet during the battle of Jutland on 31 May 1916.

Woman working as a wheel fitter, *c.* 1916. As early as 1914 women throughout Britain had decided to dedicate themselves to the war effort and, on 17 July 1915, a huge procession of women was organised by former suffragette organisations which had struggled so violently in the pre-war years to gain women the vote. There was resentment from male trade unions who feared cheap labour but the public was now ready to accept women workers.

Thousands of women entered commerce, banks and government offices. Many were employed in munitions factories and, indeed, to be a 'munitionette' became something of a status symbol. The coming of conscription increased the employment of women and many, like this chimney sweep, were now seen working in a variety of areas of daily life.

It is 1915 and these local girls are working in a Darlington shell shop.

While the men went to war the women took over their jobs: here is a tyre fitter.

Within a few months of the outbreak of the war, women were increasingly seen taking over the jobs of their fathers, husbands and sons who had volunteered or been called up. Women helped to bring in the 1914 harvest. They worked at jobs as assorted as road sweepers, shop assistants and delivery van drivers. Here local girls are shown cleaning an NER locomotive. They are doing all these jobs not because they are ardent patriots or pacifists, but because they have accepted the inevitability of war.

Sergeant Edward Cooper of Stockton, who won his Victoria Cross in 1917 during the Ypres offensive, is pictured here being congratulated by King George V after the investiture. He had fought in the battle of Passchendaele where the British second and fifth armies, with French support, sought to break out of the Ypres salient to the Belgian coast to turn the German Right and remove pressure from the beleaguered French armies to the south.

This is an artist's impression of the action in which Sergeant Edward Cooper won the VC, single-handedly capturing a blockhouse and forty-five German prisoners during the Ypres offensive in 1917.

Shown here aged 85 and with the rank of Major, Edward Cooper has lived a full life of service to the community of Stockton. Wearing his VC and other medals with justifiable pride, he realises the great debt we all owe to those who 'gave their tomorrow so that we could have our today'. Major Cooper was President of the Cleveland and Durham branch of the Royal British Legion; but he was more than that. In these days of personalities posing as heroes, he was the genuine article, a real hero, a human being of the highest order.

Major Cooper's coffin is carried into Thornaby United Reform Church for the funeral service. It is fitting that his coffin is draped in the Union Jack. Without doubt, Major Cooper has earned his place in Heaven.

If I should die, think only this of me:
That there's some corner of a foreign field
That is for ever England.
Rupert Brooke, 1887–1915
War graves at Ypres.

Having halted the massive German 1918 spring offensive, the allies mounted counter-offensives, which culminated in the pursuit of the retreating German army in October and early November. This led to the Armistice of 11 November 1918. The war now over, Flanders mud could be exchanged for home comforts. This commodity was in short supply in the Thistle Green area of Stockton, which was awaiting demolition as part of a slum clearance programme. The whole area was pulled down in about 1925 and now Stockton police station stands there.

'No more Army grub for me. When I get demobbed and am back home in Stockton, I'm going to treat myself to some real food!' Women selling crabs at Stockton Market, *c.* 1920.

The Jazz Age

Presentation of the freedom of the Borough of Stockton-on-Tees to Mr R.H. Massey, Prime Minister of New Zealand, on 20 August 1921.

Stockton Town Hall is older than the century. In 1951, when this picture was taken, the building and the nearby doric column were little changed in appearance from 1900. The size of the town hall is deceptive, being roomier inside than its exterior suggests. Apart from being the venue for town council meetings, several shopkeepers had premises there alongside law courts, a pub and a gaol.

Stockton's emblem on the council chamber windows. During a period of council intransigence in 1964, local TV personality Luke Casey suggested a new Latin inscription to go under the coat of arms: RIGOR MORTIS.

Behind Stockton High Street many mean hovels were situated in the yards, access being gained along narrow passages or wynds. This picture, which dates from 1880, illustrates the wretched conditions still prevailing in the 1920s, which led to the introduction of a large slum clearance programme.

Slum clearance is a protracted business. These dwellings on Stockton Quay were still standing in 1968 when this picture was taken. Those whose homes they were had long since been rehoused and the buildings have now been demolished.

The Quayside Mission was founded in 1906 and continued to provided a 'home' for sixty destitute men throughout the 1920s and beyond. Situated in The Square, Stockton, the building – with its gloomy passages and uncarpeted dormitories – had originally been a mission. It closed in 1973 and has now been demolished.

c. 1925. Utter despair is etched on the faces of these residents at the Quayside Mission, where maintenance was difficult when the only guaranteed income was the 25*s* a week the men paid. For this they were given a room and a bed, but provided their own meals. Five years earlier the future had seemed full of promise with soldiers who had returned from the war finding work easily. By 1921 the wartime boom was over. British markets throughout the world had disappeared, shipbuilding was no longer profitable and oil was superceding coal as a fuel. Primary industries began to suffer, huge war debts had to be repaid and unemployment reached two million. Wages fell and Lloyd George's pledge of 'homes fit for heroes' became a hollow promise. For many it was a time without hope.

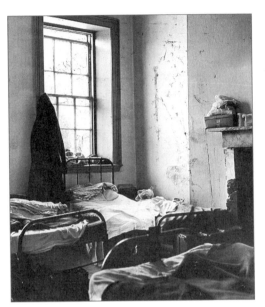

With the end of hostilities in 1918, hopes of a brighter future were expressed in a popular song 'The bells are ringing for me and my girl'. It was a short-lived dream. For many the jazz age was fun but for others it was a different story – a grey life of unemployment or soul-destroying, inadequate work. For the mostly itinerant residents of the Quayside Mission work, if it was available, was infinitely preferable to the spartan dormitories.

Whitwell's Ironworks, Thornaby, gave employment to many men from Stockton and the surrounding district. Here the ironworks and its immediate surroundings are seen from the top of a chimney during the 1920s.

Not everyone in Stockton was down and out. Most who had survived the war wanted to rebuild their lives and make the most of peace. Among the well-to-do in the 1920s, being modern was the thing. Old rules were challenged in behaviour, fashion, music and dance. Jazz became the rage and lively dances accompanied it. Hard-working women who had found independence during the war revealed new ways of dressing, drank and smoked in public and challenged the demure, ladylike manners expected of them. More and more women began to wear make-up and to frequent restaurants without a chaperone. Yet, while many celebrated the new freedom, others complained of decadence and immorality.

Those who could afford it dined out in style and the search for pleasure sometimes seemed frenzied. Risky plays were staged, erotic film stars were admired and the latest dance music crazes could be heard in millions of homes on gramophones and the wireless.

Advertising increasingly reminded people of the heights to which they could aspire. In thoroughly modern Britain the sky was the limit. Sports cars brought speed and freedom, travel brought adventure and newspapers and magazines fed the public's appetite for sensational stories. During the modern 1920s people worked hard at having fun. This theatre handbill for the Stockton Amateur Stage Society played a small part in making the Stockton of the 1920s thoroughly modern.

Where it is necessary to purchase a ticket to see the Stockton Amateur Stage Society production of Gilbert and Sullivan's comic operas, none is needed to see Romeo and Juliet in Stockton's High Street. These heads carved on a building have been affectionately nicknamed after the immortal bard's star-crossed lovers although they were not designed to represent them.

The already popular game of tennis was given an added fillip in 1920 when this trophy was presented to the Teeside Tennis League by Messrs R. & L. Ropner. The Ropner family were shipbuilders who provided employment for many local people and contributed greatly to Stockton's development. They gave Stockton its first park as a gift (see pages 6 and 48) and this provided a cricket ground, bowling green, quoits green and tennis courts for the people of the town.

During the 1920s the Grey Horse Hotel, a Flowers house, was one of several public houses in Stockton High Street. It was built in about 1885 on the site of an old coaching inn and remained in business until 1965 when, along with adjacent shops, it was auctioned for £75,000 for site redevelopment. The pub's last landlord, Charles Stockdale, took over the Grey Horse in 1942. Before that he was licensee of the Rolling Mills Arms, Portrack. He was the father of 'Gentleman Jim' Stockdale, the professional wrestler. The disappearance of the Grey Horse left Stockton High Street with nine public houses and left Flowers with three in the town.

The Theatre public house was built by a local soda manufacturer, Thomas Wright, and opened on 8 July 1870. The Theatre Royal stood nearby and in appearance they were much alike. The Theatre public house was very popular with modern 1920s theatregoers. The Theatre Royal is no more, but the Theatre continues to look after its patrons.

This gas-holder, pictured on Stockton's Northern Gas Board premises in 1971, was fully operational during the 1920s and until long after the Second World War. When natural gas was fed into the national grid, gas-holders like this one became obsolete.

During the 1920s, all Stockton's streets were lit by gas. With the coming of electricity these elegant gas lamps were replaced by stark, utilitarian electric ones. The streets were better lit; but now passers-by could see many of the streets' inadequacies which, thankfully, had remained obscure in gaslight.

47

The lake in Ropner Park continued to provide a haven of peace and relaxation as it had done since the park was opened to the public on 4 October 1883, by the Duke and Duchess of York, later King George V and Queen Mary. For many it was an escape from the harsh reality of living on the poverty line.

The trees on the lake's two islands and around its edge, photographed here in 1959, are taller than they were in the 1920s; otherwise this timeless scene has changed little.

Victoria Bridge was opened on 20 June 1887, to replace an earlier five-arch bridge. Until recent boundary changes it linked Durham with Yorkshire. Here it links the 1920s with the 1930s.

Depressive Times

Originally a tithe barn, this building was converted into a theatre by Thomas Bates in 1766 and it became Stockton's tiny Georgian Theatre, one of many provincial theatres to be built during the prosperous years of the eighteenth century. Bates owned the theatre for twenty-odd years, then sold it to a well-known actor, James Cawdell, who turned the debt-ridden theatre into a profitable enterprise. Other owners failed to match Cawdell's financial success, but the theatre remained in business, becoming known in the 1850s as the Royal. Between the mid-nineteenth century and the end of the First World War, music hall became the major leisure industry. The Georgian Theatre changed from being 'legitimate' to music hall, but this was not a success and it closed. It was converted into a Salvation Army headquarters before becoming J.F. Smith's Nebo sweet factory in the mid-1920s. One day somebody burned the peanuts. It gave them a better flavour and the result was crunchy nut toffee, which was made there during the 1930s.

The narrow alleyway which, in the 1920s, led to Nebo sweet factory. When the factory closed, much restoration work was undertaken and the premises were replaced as a theatre and exhibition centre in 1980.

Donald and James Smith founded the factory and Donald produced a cough sweet that became a household name throughout the north-east. Sacks of sugar were stored under the stage alongside roasting machines, and women in sugar-dusted overalls heaved great copper pans off the stove and poured molten toffee into trays. So the magic of the Georgian Theatre was maintained. Anyone entering what for so many years had been a theatrical dream factory would see sugar, glucose, water and a magical ingredient 'It' become transformed into a different sort of dream factory. Here, specially for children, a different kind of magic was made and it had all sorts of different names: cinder toffee, nut toffee, crunchie munchie, spearmint drops, malt bricks, mint humbugs, herbal candy, 'winter warmer' to soothe sore throats, lemon fizzes and sherbet. Sweet dreams!

During the Depression, the churches in Stockton must have provided solace for many people whose lives had become very hard. The Unitarian church in Wellington Street was one such sanctuary, pictured here in 1992.

The beautiful interior of Stockton's Baptist Tabernacle Church.

Like the well-known hymn book, these two pictures are Ancient and Modern. They clearly show the extent to which modern artists using modern materials differ from the traditional romanticism of an earlier age. The stained glass window is in Holy Trinity Church.

Here the stained glass window is pictured between two other windows of plain glass; but of the congregation there is no sign. Could the sermon really have been so dull? In 1838 Holy Trinity Church, an imposing Gothic-style church with flying buttresses, was built on land provided by Bishop van Mildert, the last of Durham's Prince Bishops. It is thought that Holy Trinity was a 'Waterloo Church', one of several built by a grateful government to commemorate the victory at Waterloo on 18 June 1815. The church was consecrated on 22 December 1838. After the Second World War, largely because of population movements, congregations shrank and the church was closed. Following its closure as a Church of England place of worship, the Greek Orthodox community used Holy Trinity until October 1991, when a devilish fire gutted the interior and put a large question mark over the building's future.

Stockton parish church is pictured here in 1935 overlooking a High Street remarkably free of traffic.

During the inter-war years traffic along High Street was intensifying. Some of Stockton's earlier buses, single and double decker, are pictured here lined up at the bus stand near the middle of the High Street in the 1930s.

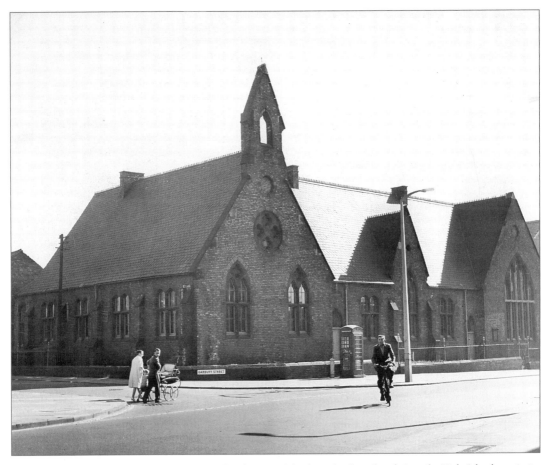

Stockton Grammar School had three precursors: the Blue Coat School, an Anglican foundation; the High School, a private, late nineteenth-century venture; and the old Grammar School on Garbutt Street, pictured here in 1961. From there the present school has inherited ideals of faith and service, and academic standards. Between 1920 and 1930 the number of pupils on the old Grammar School roll averaged 150 and life was very diversified with an increase of school societies and other activities. But in 1929 the Board indicated that the buildings were unsatisfactory and that the alternatives open to the governors were closure or the provision of a new building. In 1930 a new head, Mr Ridley, was appointed and steps were taken to increase the number of pupils and improve the financial standing of the school. By 1934 a strong movement in the town, and particularly among the governors, argued that closure should not be accepted as a certainty and that the school should be remodelled. It was feared, however, that because of a proposed new secondary school, the county council would withdraw its grant. The council made it quite clear to the school governors that there was no reason to assume that the grant would cease when their own enlarged school was built.

In consequence, the years 1935 and 1936 were very hectic. Plans were drawn up to remodel completely and extend the school on its existing site to accommodate between 180 and 200 boys. Thus from 1936 the buildings remained substantially unchanged until they were vacated in April 1963.

Ropner Park was tastefully landscaped: the broader avenues were straight but all the plants were set down in a series of curves. Some of the flower beds were raised both for artistic effect and to act as windbreaks. The one shown here depicts King George VI and Queen Elizabeth in floral profile with the crown, to celebrate his coronation on 12 May 1937.

In 1976, in celebration of the invention of the friction match 150 years earlier, the town's Parks Department produced this remarkable floral tribute to Stockton's Matchman. Depicted in the display are a flaming match, a pestle and mortar. It is a fitting tribute to John Walker and a credit to Stockton's Parks Department whose high standard of floral art matches that of the 1930s.

Gardener Ray Hewitson, right, and Mike Langley, the technical officer who designed this display, are shown here in July 1976, photographing their creation. Stockton is rightly proud of John Walker who was born there in 1781. Between 1819 and 1858 he worked as a chemist and druggist at 59 High Street. In 1826 he invented the friction match but did not patent his invention, leaving others to gain fame and fortune from his work.

War clouds had been gathering throughout the 1930s and the future looks grim. But life goes on and Stockton's High Street market traders bring a sense of normality to an increasingly unstable world. It is 3 May 1939 and conflict with Germany is on the horizon.

An extension of the scene opposite on the same day. Increasing traffic problems on Stockton High Street have resulted in the introduction for the first time of road signs. The war put projects like this on hold and changed the lives of all the people shown here.

'Dig for Victory', first launched in a broadcast of October 1939 by the Agriculture Minister, Sir Reginald Dorman-Smith, called for every able-bodied man and woman to dig an allotment in their spare time. Lawns and flower-beds were turned into vegetable gardens, the aim being to make Britain as self-sufficient as possible. It was one of the greatest of wartime slogans. Stockton, along with the rest of Britain, prepared for austerity.

"I've been trying to make up my mind whether she's showing too much light."

A blackout was imposed throughout the land and along the streets of Stockton, as elsewhere, a new cry was heard: an ARP warden shouting 'Put that ruddy light out!' British humour finds laughter in the most unlikely situations, as this cartoon illustrates. Humour and song played a very important part in winning the war. 'Run, Rabbit, Run,' which was paraphrased to 'Run, Adolf, Run,' and 'Wish Me Luck as You Wave Me Goodbye', were two of the hit songs of 1939.

The Fighting Forties

In Stockton, as elsewhere, people 'made do' by mending old clothes with a needle and thread, scrap materials from rags to waste paper were collected for reprocessing, bones were salvaged to make glue for aircraft, scrap metals and aluminium were collected to make fighter planes like the Spitfire and ornamental iron railings were sacrificed to make ships and tanks.

Many windows in
Stockton were taped or
papered against bomb
blast; and advice on
home defence against
air raids was illustrated
on cigarette cards and
elsewhere.

Everyone was issued with an identity
card, containing a personal number,
which had to be carried at all times
and produced on demand. Other
personal documents issued were a
Ministry of Food Ration Book, which
was handed to the shopkeeper along
with the appropriate amount of cash
for the purchase of restricted food.
The shopkeeper would cut out the
required number of coupons, which
he needed to replenish his stocks. If
no coupons remained in the Ration
Book for the appropriate period, only
unrationed food could be purchased.
Spivs overcame this difficulty by
providing an illegal 'black market'
where no coupons were needed, but
over-the-odds prices were charged.
Food shortages lasted long after the
war ended, as can be seen by the
dates on the Ration Book shown
here. Clothes were also rationed.

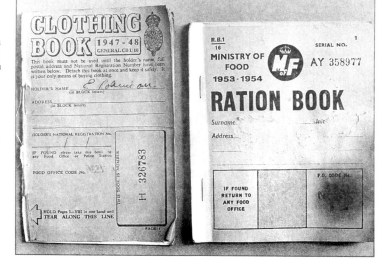

The Women's Land Army was one of the options Stockton's girls had as their contribution to the war effort; and those who joined spent the war years working on farms throughout the country. There was no official evacuation of Stockton's children although private arrangements were made by some families for their youngsters to be boarded out with country relatives. On the face of it, this seemed odd because of the huge ICI chemicals complex and heavy industrial works on the doorstep; and the reason was bizarre. During the 1930s a vast amount of German money had been poured into expanding ICI. Von Ribbentrop often visited the area and it is thought that it was on his orders that Teesside was spared sustained air raids.

While some Stockton girls chose to work on the land others joined the female branches of the forces: ATS, WAAF, WRNS. In May 1940, War Minister Anthony Eden called for a new defence force to be set up. It was originally known as the Local Defence Volunteers and its recruits were between seventeen and sixty-five years of age, the only fitness requirements being that they were 'capable of free movement'. Within a week a quarter of a million men joined and by July 1940 the numbers had doubled. At Churchill's suggestion the LDV was renamed the Home Guard. The Stockton branch was kept busy keeping watch on public buildings, roads and railways and looking out for parachuting enemy invaders, while those who passed their medical and had been called up joined their chosen branches of the British war machine. For some it was the Army. Here four 'Desert Rats', part of Monty's 8th Army, relax in the Western Desert during a lull in the fighting in 1941. Their oven is made from a jerrycan, washing is done in petrol and no bedrolls are laid out in case they have to leave in a hurry.

Some Stockton men joined the RAF. This photograph shows 431 Squadron's daylight raid on a VI construction site at Gorenflos, near Abbeville, on 28 June 1944. Squadron 431 was based at Croft, about 13 miles west of Stockton.

Others joined the Royal Navy and some served on convoy duty around the world. They did a fine job of it as this 1945 message recognises.

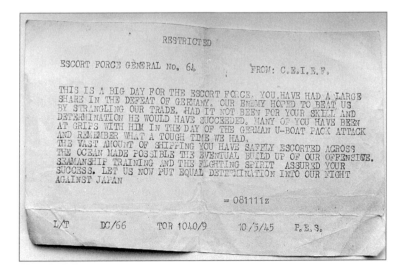

On 8 May 1945, the Prime Minister, Winston Churchill, broadcast a victory message to millions of listeners in Great Britain and throughout the British Commonwealth. He said 'Yesterday morning at 2.41 a.m. at Headquarters, General Jodl, the representative of the German High Command, and Grand Admiral Donitz, the designated head of the German State, signed the pact of unconditional surrender of all German land, sea and air forces in Europe to the Allied Expeditionary Force and simultaneously to the Russian High Command. . . . We may allow ourselves a brief period of rejoicing, but let us not forget for a moment the toil and efforts that lie ahead. Japan, with all her treachery and greed, remains unsubsided. . . . We must now devote all our strength and resources to the completion of our task at home and abroad. Advance Britannia! Long live the cause of Freedom! God save the King!'

On 8 May 1945, along with the rest of Great Britain, the people of Stockton celebrated and the *Northern Echo* recorded this momentous historical event.

The first victory salute.

In Stockton and throughout the land the street parties began, 1945. In the small hours of 7 May 1945 General Alfred Jodl signed an unconditional surrender. Hitler was already dead and Germany had acknowledged defeat. Prime Minister, Winston Churchill, and US President, Harry S. Truman, agreed that the following day, 8 May, should be celebrated as Victory in Europe (VE) day. The BBC confirmed the news and Winston Churchill broadcast to the nation at 3 p.m. That night the street lights were switched on all over Britain for the first time since the outbreak of war. It was like fairyland, especially for children. Despite war weariness, and the prospect of more austerity ahead, 'peace had broken out'. If ever there was a time to celebrate this was it.

Wartime packs of Crystella, pure dried eggs, powdered milk, blended starch and Jiffy dyes: the domestic side of war that Stockton knew so well.

'Lilli Marlene', the German song adopted by the Allies, Vera Lynn, Bill Cotton, the quickstep, the foxtrot: all part of the romantic, sentimental face of war, not often seen, which was essential to the morale of the fighting forces and civilians alike.

65

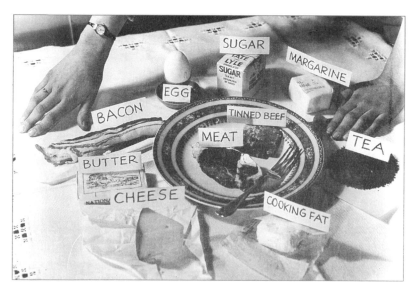

This is one person's ration in 1945. Anyone buying an 'all day breakfast' in a Stockton eatery today will expect, and get, a more varied meal than this week's ration would provide.

But who cares about food rationing when there is a regular supply of the brown stuff? Here, at the Sun Inn, Stockton, a regular customer shares a joke or two and a few jars with his mates.

The King's Message of Congratulation

THE Editor, Mr. Ashley S. Standbol received the following letter from Sandringham in reply to a message of loyal greeting sent to HIM the King from the Darlington and Stockton Times on the occasion of its centenary.

Dear Sir—I am commanded by the King to thank you for your letter of the 26th September in which you conveyed a message of loyal greetings to His Majesty from the proprietors, editor, manager and staff of the "Darlington and Stockton Times" on the occasion of its centenary on October 4th next.

His Majesty has greatly interested to learn of the landmark in the history of your paper and trusts that the record of its usefulness, the completion of one hundred years of uninterrupted publication and that the past will accord its continuation of this impressive record in provincial journalism.

Yours truly,
EDMUND HOOD
Assistant Private Secretary

FOREWORD
BY THE EDITOR.

DARLINGTON
PUBLIC LIBRARY.

A proud record in provincial journalism was reached on October 4th, 1947, when the centenary issue of the "Darlington and Stockton Times" was published. In celebration of the event lunches were held at focal points in each of six large edition areas — Darlington, Stockton, Northallerton, Thirsk, Ripon and Barnard Castle.

The centenary lunches were attended by leading personalities in the public, business and professional life of the North Riding of Yorkshire and County Durham and notable tributes were expressed in appreciation of the services rendered by the "Darlington and Stockton Times" to town and country communities throughout the area of circulation. Many scores of congratulatory messages were received from readers.

The purpose of this publication is to outline the manner in which the "Darlington and Stockton Times" commemorated its 100th anniversary. Its pages reveal the romantic rise of the newspaper to recognition as one of the leading provincial weekly organs in the country and reflect the prestige it holds in the North-East.

Two memorable events helped Stockton people to forget for a while the dull, dingy, depressing post-war years. The first was the 100th birthday of the *Darlington & Stockton Times* on 4 October 1947, when King George VI sent the paper a congratulatory letter. During its first century the *D & S Times* has flourished and is held in high regard by its discerning readership.

The second was the return of a little bit of glamour, following six years of wartime austerity. 'Don't you know there's a war on?', had become 'Don't you know there's peace on?', spoken with just a hint of one-upmanship by fashion-conscious young Stockton ladies in their new outfits.

As the twentieth century approached its halfway point, India celebrated its independence (at midnight on 14/15 August 1947), HRH Princess Elizabeth married Lt Philip Mountbatten (20 November 1947), Gandhi was assassinated (30 January 1948), the National Health Service came into operation (5 July 1948), the 14th Olympiad took place at Wembley (29 July–14 August 1948), Prince Charles was christened at Buckingham Palace (16 December 1948) and sweet rationing ended (24 April 1949) – but stocks were soon exhausted and sweet rationing was resumed (14 August 1949). It was against this background that Stockton girded itself to deal with the formidable tasks ahead, among them slum clearance and the neglect of the war years. While Stockton's eyes were on the future, those who had made the supreme sacrifice in defence of freedom were held in sacred memory. Every Remembrance Sunday the famous words of war poet Laurence Binyon, written in 1914, were spoken at Stockton's cenotaph, 'They shall not grow old as we that are left grow old: Age shall not weary them, nor the years condemn. At the going down of the sun and in the morning, we will remember them.'

The Teenage Fifties

Jimmy James was a giant of the music hall, a comedian's comedian, who in a recent poll was voted British comedian of the century, ahead of other established favourites like Morecambe and Wise. His real name was James Casey and he was born in Stockton in 1892. He began as a juvenile performer, 'Terry – the Blue-eyed Irish Boy', but after being gassed in the First World War found that he could no longer sing, so he turned to comedy. Never a drinker himself, Jimmy James developed his hilarious drunk sketches, added stooges and became a real original, building up a repertoire of beautifully crafted and superbly executed sketches. The delightfully choreographed movements between himself, Eli Woods and Roy Castle were a joy to watch and the inspired lunacy of their logic in classic sketches like 'First Night', 'The Shoebox', 'Sober as a Judge' and 'The Spare Room', touched the giddy heights of surrealistic splendour. Twice he was brought to the London Palladium, variety's Mecca, to save the day: once when Arthur Lucan and Kitty McShane, Old Mother Riley and her daughter, flopped there, and again when Mickey Rooney died a death there. He did one Royal Variety Performance in 1953 and stopped the show. He was loved and admired by many thousands of fans who shared his surreal yet totally acceptable world. He died in 1965; and his BBC producer son, James Casey, and his nephew, the real Eli Woods, have been doing his 'Shoebox' act again. It really is a bit special.

Jack Casey, a famous son of Stockton, is the nephew of Jimmy James, and as Eli Woods was his most famous stooge. In the classic sketch about the lion in the shoebox he and Roy Castle both wore huge hats and coats that reached to the ground. Eli was a superb feed with immaculate timing. He was very lanky – he still is – with a contrived stutter. He would invariably intersperse his opening words in a sketch with a series of fah! fah! fahs! while trying to establish that it was not Jimmy James who had been 'putting it about that I'm barmy'. To stage drunk and real life teetotaller Jimmy James, Jack Casey was 'Our Eli'; and their head-bobbing routines were a joy to watch. Uncle and nephew worked together until the summer of 1964 when Jimmy James collapsed at Skegness, dying the following year.

In their act, Jimmy James and Eli Woods always included two imaginary characters, Hutton Conyers (a village in Yorkshire) and Bretton Woods (the New Hampshire venue for the 1944 United Nations Financial Conference), which did these places no harm at all. But the special place that proudly reflected their successes was never used in their sketches – Stockton-on-Tees.

Teenage Teddy Boys and their girls jiving at local hops were the flavour of the 1950s and illustrated how times were changing. Where, in the 1930s, shy youths seated at one side of a dance hall would cross it to ask one of a row of shy young things 'for the pleasure of the next dance', the more confident Teds of the 1950s, usually gathered in groups, would grab a girl with a 'Hi worm, let's squirm' and, held at arms length, they would jive. Today they don't hold hands – even in Stockton.

71

This is Stockton's original market seen from the clock tower with the Doric Monument in the foreground. It is the 1950s and the stalls have not changed much with the years; but the traffic has. Double-decker buses are prominent and pedestrian crossings have been introduced.

The High Street from the north in the mid-1950s, showing the car parking and the bus stands.

The Permissive Years

This picture, taken on 19 November 1968, sheds some light on Stockton's sometimes bloodthirsty past. The young lady is holding a poster advertising cockfighting at Stockton's Black Lion Hotel in 1790. It was found at the bottom of an old trunk at the hotel; and the rich prize money shows the popularity of the sport at that time.

In 1966, the year the Rank organisation announced record pre-tax profits of £19 million, plans were already afoot to redevelop the east side of the High Street. The Rank Organisation, which thought that an old theatre in the middle of a new development area would look odd, decided to close the old Odeon (shown here) and replace it with a modern version. The last film shown at the old Odeon before it was demolished was *Lt Robin Crusoe USN*. This 2,100-seat cinema, originally named the Regal, was opened in 1935. The Rank organisation took it over in 1945 and renamed it the Odeon.

The new Odeon opened in 1967 on the original site at a cost of £250,000. Mr Goldthorpe, who had managed Stockton's old Odeon since 1954. The new Odeon had a smaller seating capacity than the original one but incorporated the latest cinematographic developments and provided maximum comfort for cinema-goers.

The Globe Theatre, a popular venue for Stockton's music hall and variety buffs, had a theatre bar. When the Globe became a cinema and its name was change to the ABC, the theatre bar, pictured here on 22 June 1965,

Between the demolition of Stockton's old Odeon and the building of the new Odeon the ABC was the only cinema in town. Typical of the films shown there during the 1960s were *Psycho* in 1962, *Hello Dolly* in 1964, and *King of the Road* in 1965. With flower power all the rage and 'make love not war' being the thing to do, snogging in the semi-dark of a cinema auditorium became *de rigueur*. A pop song of the early 1960s caught the flavour of changing attitudes: 'Fings Ain't Wot They Used to Be'.

Stockton's Hippodrome on the corner of Dovecot Street and Prince Regent Street was built in 1905. During the 88 years of its existence it was renamed the Classic, then the Essoldo and finally the Cannon. It began as a theatre, then, following a fire on 8 November 1932, reopened as a cinema. In the immediate post-war years it reverted to variety but ended its days as a cinema.

The magic of the silver screen at Stockton's Empire began its appeal during the 1950s. In November 1961 the cinema was reduced to holding an auction of memorabilia. As this poignant picture shows, even Lady Chatterley's certificate X days are over. Her expression is wistful, but perhaps she has few regrets.

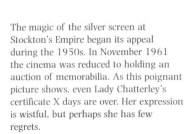

80

One of the reasons the Rank organisation decided to replace the old Odeon with a new, modernised Odeon was that a spanking new post office was to be built to the left of the cinema. The then mayor of Stockton, is seen opening the new post office on 2 December 1960.

Stockton's new civic centre, 1961.

Photographed on 29 March 1960, part of the wall at St Chad's Church, Stockton, with the figure of St Chad built into it.

This 15 ft long bronze, fibre-glass figure of Christ still dominates one of the largest housing estates in Stockton. It was manoeuvred into position on the eastern wall of Hardwick's modern parish church, St James', which was built during the 1960s to serve the new estate. This took place on 17 March 1967 and, despite gusts of wind of up to 70 mph, there were no mishaps.

Before the statue of Christ (above right) could be put in position, the church of St James' had to be built. Here it is under construction, 31 January 1961.

On 19 September 1961, the foundation stone of Stockton's new £150,000 Grammar School, a Church of England foundation, was laid by the Rt Revd Maurice Harland, DD, Lord Bishop of Durham. At 2.30 on Friday 11 October 1963, the most Revd and Rt Hon. Donald Coggan, DD, Archbishop of York, officiated at the dedication of the new Grammar School and the hallowing of the chapel.

The Rt Revd Mgr J.J. Cunningham, Vicar-General of Hexham and Newcastle opened the new St Mary's Catholic Girls Secondary School in 1965. The school itself claims to be one of the oldest in Stockton teaching the Catholic religion. It was sited in Major Street before 1850. Until 1870 it was an all-age school for girls and boys. In 1872 the sisters of Charity of St Paul the Apostle taught the girls. The school was demolished in 1910 and a new school was built on the site. When the girls moved to Bishopton Lane West, they were housed in five different buildings in the area. In September 1972, St Bede's Roman Catholic Boys School and St Mary's Girls School amalgamated. The new school became Our Lady and St Bede's Comprehensive.

Housing development in Stockton, 1961. Here new houses are replacing buildings that have passed their sell-by date.

A year later, in 1962, Stockton still has its mean areas. Children play in a grim street and an empty gasometer stands stark against a dull winter sky.

Typical shop frontages on Stockton's High Street, 1966. During the first half of the twentieth century an even richer diversity of shops had brought colour and, more importantly, shoppers from a wide catchment area to Stockton High Street. The Public Benefit Boot Company used to make and sell footwear, A. Curry & Sons were butchers, W. Scorer was an ironmonger and R. Scupman & Son made picture frames. Millers was a candy store and Lamplughs was a hosiery and wool shop. All these, and many more at different times, have now gone and with them a lot of trade captured by out-of-town supermarkets.

This unusual view along one of Stockton's alleys, pictured on 5 July 1962, highlights the great appeal of the town's narrow passages.

It is 18 November 1968, and the ladies beneath the poultry at Stockton Market are Mrs Gladys Meynell, right, and Mrs Freda Eden, both from Welbury, Northallerton, both of whom get up at 4 a.m. to get to market on time.

Two days earlier, on 16 November 1968, a stallholder at Stockton Market carries a gas lamp to her stall in the poor dawn light.

Above: The £5 million development scheme for the east side of Stockton's famous High Street, long bedevilled by repeated hold-ups, got the go-ahead following a visit to the town on 26 October 1967 by a deputation from the Royal Fine Art Commission from London, the body which blocked the original plan and asked for certain revisions to it. Here the three-man Commission, led by Lord Holford, its chairman, is inspecting the High Street. Later the Commission met the local development plan sub-committee, responsible for the redevelopment. Thanks to these people, Stockton cinema-goers got a new Odeon and the High Street got a face-lift.

Meanwhile the big M came to Stockton High Street: mounting car numbers.

Recognising a bargain when they see one, in 1969 these canny Stockton housewives still let the Municipal Launderette take the strain out of the weekly wash.

Happy Railway Anniversary

Throughout the 1970s, one event towered above all others in Stockton and caught the imagination of all Britain. It was the 150th anniversary of the opening of the Stockton & Darlington Railway in 1825. Actually, the railway age began three years earlier, during the afternoon of Thursday 23 May 1822, when 300 shouting, singing navvies dragged a carriage carrying one of the local dignitaries into Stockton where, at St John's Well, he laid the first rail of the S&DR. Afterwards everyone sang 'God Save The King', then the dignitaries, including Mr Meynell, first chairman of the S&DR, and George Stephenson went to the mayor's reception and the navvies dined on bread, cheeses and ale at the Black Lion Inn. The S&DR was not the world's first public railway – the Loughborough and Nanpanton was, in 1789. It was not the first steam railway – the Penydarren Colliery line, South Wales, which carried VIP passengers at its opening, was. It was not the first passenger train – the Swansea and Mumbles in 1806 was. It was not even the first railway instituted by an Act of Parliament – the Middleton Railway, Leeds, 1785, which switched entirely to steam in 1812, holds that distinction. But it was the first public railway worked by steam, although for several years after the gala opening of 1825 its steam traction was reserved for freight.

A rare Stockton & Darlington Railway Company £25 share certificate.

The S&DR booked its first passenger on 27 September 1825.

The world's first railway ticket office at St John's crossing, Stockton.

Don Pearson, booking office clerk at Stockton Railway station, booked the last passenger on 18 July 1988.

A replica of Stephenson's *Locomotion*, pictured here on 25 August 1975, pulling a chaldron wagon and a coach, leading the Rail Cavalcade at Shildon to mark the 150th anniversary of the opening of the S&DR.

Here the S&DR 150th anniversary cavalcade is being marshalled at Shildon. In all thirty-five engines took part, including the latest BR high-speed train. Leading the line-up in this picture is LNWR 'Precedent' class 2–4–0, No. 790, *Hardwicke*, which was introduced in 1873. In the summer of 1895, at the time of intense rivalry between the West Coast (London & North Western Railway and the Caledonian Railway) and the East Coast route (Great Northern Railway, North Eastern Railway and the North British Railway), *Hardwicke* raced the section from Crewe to Carlisle. Her finest performance was on 22 August 1895, when she covered 141 miles in 126 minutes.

Gordon, class 9F, 2–10–0, seen here on 25 August 1975, was the second locomotive of its class, 'Austerity', to be built by the Ministry of Supply for use by the British Army on the Longmoor Military Railway in Hampshire for instructional purposes. It was introduced in 1943 and named after General Gordon of Khartoum. Its wartime livery was blue. It is seen here as part of the S&DR 150th anniversary cavalcade towing London transport Electric No. 12, *Sarah Siddons*.

Green Arrow, seen here on the line between Shildon and Heighington during the anniversary cavalcade on 25 August 1975, is a class V2, 2–6–2, locomotive, No. 4771, built in 1936. It is one of five constructed as forerunners of a new class designed to meet increasing demands for fast, reliable, mixed traffic locomotives. At the outbreak of the Second World War almost 100 class V2s were in service and LNER crews called them 'the locomotive that won the war'. In total 182 were built.

In 1975, the Post Office issued a commemorative set of stamps to mark the development of railways from Stephenson's *Locomotion*, through the steam era to today's less romantic but much more expensive high-speed train.

Stockton Railway station in 1978 and, sadly, not a train in sight.

The £4.5 million redevelopment of the south-east side of Stockton's High Street, near the Doric Column, began with the demolition of some of the town's historic buildings. Thousands watched the buildings fall to the blows of battering rams and saw familiar shops vanish by the lorry-load as rubble. Then came the levelling, seen here in July 1970.

A year on and the redevelopment is well advanced.

The fourth estate is absolutely essential to a community and Teesside is exceptionally well endowed in this respect. As befitted a market town serving a large population, Stockton needed a newspaper that would be readily acceptable to such a diverse readership. On 2 October 1847, the splendid weekly *The Darlington & Stockton Times* was launched. When the *Northern Echo*, the world's first halfpenny morning newspaper, was founded at Darlington in 1870 by J. Hyslop Bell it found a large readership in and around Stockton. A new dimension was added when in 1971 Radio Teesside started life in Linthorpe Road, Middlesbrough. A black door bearing the station's name is all passers-by saw of the station, but upstairs were two floors with a production office, two studios, offices and a workshop for the three engineers it took to maintain the equipment. At first the station was only on VHF, but in time it gained a medium wave frequency and began to make its mark in Teesside, South Durham and North Yorkshire. Here presenters (left to right) Mike Hollingworth, John Watson and Colin Bunyan are seen in front of the new broadcasting house opposite Middlesbrough Bus Station.

The first team was led by Allan Shaw with Jim Brady as his deputy and Ian Hindmarsh who ran the news operation. An essential piece of equipment was the outside broadcast car. In 1974 Radio Teesside became Cleveland and her OB car carries the new title.

Peter Duncan, left, and Stewart McFarlane doing an outside broadcast in 1985.

Presenter Matthew Davies.

Presenter Sue Sweeney.

Presenter Alan Wright.

Presenter Ken Snowdon.

Broadcasting House, the home of Radio Cleveland, the voice of Teesside since 1980. This magnificent building in Newport Road, Middlesbrough, was designed by architect Malcolm Cundick. From here BBC Radio Cleveland will ring in the new millennium.

The Enlightening Eighties

As in the 1970s, so in the 1980s, Stockton High Street's open market remains constant in an ever-changing environment.

The River Tees has always played an important part in the life of Stockton. Between the Princess of Wales Bridge and, upstream, the Surtees Road Bridge that carries the A66 over the Tees, are the sites of Cork Insulations and Asbestos Co., Teesdale Wharf and Whitwells Quay, Malleable Wharf, Richardson Dock and Co. shipyard that was taken over by Head Wrightson, Craig Taylor and Co. Shipyard, Blair's Sheerlegs, Ropner's Shipyard and Fitting-out Quay, Bishop's Landing and Kelly's Ferry Corporation, Castle and Railway Wharfs coal staithes, Cleveland Flour Mill silo, Teesside Bottle Plant, Vulcan Ironworks, Bousefield Steelworks, Tees Bridge Ironworks and Richmond Ironworks. Here, pictured in 1986, is Stockton Power Station.

Here, in December 1981, four water-fowl swim among ice floes beneath Victoria Bridge close to small craft.

The old order changeth . . . old buildings have been demolished and the riverside site levelled. It is August 1988, and a fair will be held on the site in 1989.

Fireworks burst over the Tees during the 1989 Festival. Stockton's International Festival began in 1987 as a community event and has grown tremendously since then. It now incorporates a very popular community carnival, street theatre with acts from around the world, music for all tastes and artistry. Its pyrotechnics constantly win acclaim and it is one of Europe's leading festivals of street theatre attracting more than 40,000 people annually. The Festival has also become an established venue for international circuses and, for the Millennium, circuses performing at several Cleveland venues will merge with that at the Stockton Festival to form Circus 2000 – predicted to be out of this world!

This huge artificial cob-swan being paraded through Stockton, as part of the town's 1988 Festival, symbolises Stockton's continuing transition from ugly duckling to beautiful swan.

In 1988 Stockton won a top award in the 'Britain in Bloom' competition. Albena Todorova of the 'Natcho Ivanov' ensemble from Sofia, Bulgaria, pictured on 17 August 1988, is looking at a floral display in one of Stockton's parks that helped to win the award.

Having fun is catching at Stockton's Market Fair, held in August 1987. Here, left to right, Maurine Powles as Boadicea, Mr and Mrs Platts, Mayor and Mayoress of Stockton, mace-bearer Bill Alderson and local historian Tom Sowler with the handbell, ring in the laughter.

In April 1987, Mary Armstrong and Gordon Rigby bring the flavour of the wholesome side of apple-pie America to Stockton. They are the GI Jumping Jivers.

Stockton High Street, pictured here on 10 December 1980, now has a bus lane and two lanes for other vehicles each side of the central area where the market stalls stand. The pedestrian crossing is in two halves: one with pedestrian-controlled lights, the other with Belisha beacons.

In July 1983, parents, fearing for the safety of their children crossing busy Norton Avenue, demanded a pelican crossing. 'We want a pelican' says the banner. A wonderful bird is a pelican, Holds as much in its beak as its belly can, Holds as much in its beak as will last him a week, And I don't know how the hell he can.

The Mayor of Stockton, Councillor Reddican, it would appear, has been listening to Norman Tebbit telling of how he got on his bike to look for work, thought it a good idea and decided to set an example. Actually Councillor Reddican heads young riders after opening Stockton's new cycleway.

During excavations for a new road along Stockton's riverside an anchor was unearthed. Here, on 31 August 1984, having been restored to its former glory, it is being placed on display alongside the Tees.

A community service team in Stockton parish church in December 1986. The vicar said there were bats in the belfry but from the look of the workers' clothing a large flock of pigeons is more likely.

Far better be a culture vulture like Ann Russell, who was Stockton's Group Librarian in 1987, or a bookworm.

Cutting the ribbon at the new Silver Court Shopping Centre on 12 December 1988, with, from the left, developer Stuart Monk, Mayor Cllr Winifred Hodgson and Nik Duncan, owner of CHIPS computer shop, one of the new stores in the centre.

Improvements to Stockton's High Street continued. Here, in 1989, developers Graham Thomas and Alexander Machachlan, with John Scott, Stockton's planning committee chairman between them, stand in front of Dressers. In 1971 this friendly bookshop and stationers opened in Stockton, becoming a welcome haven for shoppers who appreciated that personal service and old world charm are often missing in today's superstores, where customer consideration seems of little account. Stockton book-lovers could have a good browse in Dressers – now, sadly, no more. They can still have a good browse in Dressers, but have to travel 12 miles to Darlington to do so.

On 17 December 1981, the Noble Organisation opened a new amusement centre in Stockton's High Street. Don Estelle is seen here with Mrs Isobel Close of Stockton.

Amusement arcades have no appeal to a little guy who just wants to go fishing. For a toddler after tiddlers the lake in Ropner Park is the place to be. Pictured on 27 July 1989, David Rafferty is casting his net, expecting a bite and fish fingers for tea. Nobody has told him that fish do not have fingers. It is a cruel world.

Fin de Siècle

It is 9 August 1994, and Stockton's festival has a French flavour. The fireworks clock is a reminder that for the twentieth century the sands of time are running out.

These exotic gymnasts bring a touch of eastern splendour to Stockton's 1998 festival with their speciality dancing.

Stockton people know how to enjoy themselves, but they also realise that their freedom was hard won. Here, on the 50th anniversary of VE-Day, patriotic Stocktonian John Brown proudly dips the Union Jack in homage.

What did you do in the war, Gran? I was in the ATS/WRNS/WAAF/a nurse/a land army girl. Who won? We did. See this flag? It's the greatest flag in the whole wide world. Let's wave it. Whee! Stockton ladies from the left, Hazel Watson, Kathleen Sutherson, Norma Southern and Sheila Powson on the anniversary of VE-Day.

Pupils from Holy Trinity Primary School, Stockton, went back in time on 6 October 1994, at the Market Cross in the High Street, as part of their historical education.

High-wire walker Carl Carlin and pyrotechnic expert Miklos Menis (right), who sadly died in an accident in July 1999, survey the scene of a high-wire walk over Stockton High Street. Stockton parish church is clearly seen on the right where the street narrows. Carl walked the wire in August 1994. It will not catch on. Imagine carrying two heavy bags full of shopping along it on a wet, windy night.

Stockton's thoroughly modern High Street seen here in 1994 complete with pedestrian-controlled lights and, near the town hall, a pedestrian area. There is not a high wire in sight although Stockton still has the distinction of having the widest high street in the country.

'Queen Victoria' and 'Prince Bertie' welcome new residents at Wimpey's Victoria Lock development in the mid 1990s. Victoria Lock is built on land where Mrs Thatcher made her famous walk into the wilderness in 1987, following her general election victory. Old Teesside has gone and will never return – and the future is bright.

The Tees Barrage under construction, pictured on 23 July 1993. It cost £50 million to build and transformed an 11-mile stretch of the river into a lake; and allied to water quality improvements the scheme also made Teesside a major water sports centre, including a world-class canoe slalom. Building the barrage at Blue House Point, Stockton, was one of the biggest construction projects in Britain. Work started on it in 1992. Construction was carried out in eight phases and entailed diverting the Tees.

The Victoria Lock development in 1992. Roseberry Toppin' and the North York Moors are clearly seen in the background.

The £14.5 million University College of Durham's Stockton campus, which opened in 1992. This aerial view was taken on 15 June 1993. It is the biggest higher education development of its type in Britain for twenty years. The Stockton campus, both a teaching and residential site, has developed in response to local need. The Teesside region has one of the lowest higher education take-up rates in the UK, 19 full-time students per 1,000 population in Teesside compared to 42 in Tyneside and Sunderland. Durham and Teesside universities have worked together to attract more local applicants, and the Stockton operation is a key feature in that process.

In 1997–8 the Stockton campus had more than 9,000 full-time undergraduates, including 450 first years, compared with 190 in 1992 when the building opened. About half of the intake is from the region, and about a third is made up of mature students. The existing halls of residence have space for 235 students.

University College from the River. It currently offers degree courses in five main areas: Biomedical Science, Education – initial teacher training, Environmental Science, European Studies (active links with 37 European universities) and Human Sciences. The excellent facilities at the Stockton site are also attracting extra conference business to the area.

On 21 June 1995, 138 students from the University College of Stockton celebrated their exam results with a parade through Stockton High Street to the parish church.

University of Teesside graduate Paula Makepiece on 21 June 1995, showing off her graduation gown.

A good result in the exams is cause for celebration, probably in one of Stockton's fine pubs such as the Royal Exchange.

The Princess of Wales bridge under construction. Pictured on 22 February 1992, the first of two supports is in position in the photograph above and, four months later (below) the bridge is taking shape. It was opened by Princess Diana on 23 September 1992. When she was killed in a road accident, on 31 August 1997, the bridge was garlanded with hundreds of bunches of flowers – a spontaneous outpouring of emotion by generous, concerned Stocktonians.

An aerial view of Teesdale development site on 15 June 1993, with the Princess Diana Bridge complete.

A view upstream from the Tees Barrage showing the Princess Diana Bridge. The Teesdale Way, a long-distance footpath, edges the Tees on the right.

Stockton Castle, really a fortified manor house, is mentioned in the Boldon Book, a survey published by Bishop Puiset in 1183. It was an impressive structure with a moat and earthworks, but had little or no military significance; it was built as a place for entertaining and as an occasional residence.

Acknowledgements and Picture Credits

For allowing me to explore the *Northern Echo* picture library, a most enjoyable and informative occupation, my very special thanks to David Kelly, managing director of the *Northern Echo* and to Peter Barron, editor of this great newspaper. Thanks also to Peter Chapman and two intelligent ladies of great charm and loveliness, Jane Whitfield and Christine Watson, who guard the *Echo* archives and make good coffee. To the Worshipful the Mayor of Stockton-on-Tees, Cllr Mrs Jean Kitchen, sincere thanks for your co-operation on this venture. Mark Rowland-Jones of Stockton Museum Services, it is always a pleasure working with you: many thanks. David Steel, editor of BBC Radio Cleveland and Kerry Sillett, events and promotions assistant at Radio Cleveland, your contribution to the book has been of great value and I thank you for your help. Thanks also to ABC Television Pictures for permission to use the Jimmy James picture. Thank you, Ellen Rutter, for the typing. It is good to know that the editorial side is in the safe hands of a brilliant team at Sutton Publishing, editors Simon Fletcher, Anne Bennett, Alison Flowers and Joyce Percival and PR specialist Rebecca Nicholls. What a pleasure it is, working with such lovely friends! If I have overlooked anyone it is inadvertent, and I apologise. If you find any errors, they belong to me.